DRAWING FANTASY ART

HOW TO DRAW
WITCHES AND
WIZARDS

Steve Beaumont

PowerKiDS
press.
New York

Published in 2008 by The Rosen Publishing Group, Inc.
29 East 21st Street, New York, NY 10010

Artwork and text: Steve Beaumont
Editor (Arcturus): Alex Woolf
Editor (Rosen): Jennifer Way
Designer: Jane Hawkins

Library of Congress Cataloging-in-Publication Data

Beaumont, Steve.
  How to draw witches and wizards / Steve Beaumont.
      p. cm. — (Drawing fantasy art)
  Includes index.
  ISBN-13: 978-1-4042-3857-2 (library binding)
  ISBN-10: 1-4042-3857-3 (library binding)
 1. Witches in art—Juvenile literature. 2. Wizards in art—Juvenile literature.
 3. Drawing—Technique—Juvenile literature. I. Title.
  NC825.W58B43 2008
  743.4—dc22

                         2007001621

Printed in China

Contents

Introduction

With its exciting heroes and fantasy, the sword-and-sorcery genre has attracted many fans just like you. You may have watched the movies, read the books, and played the games, but have you ever created your own fantasy characters? This book will teach you how to draw your own witches and wizards!

The characters in fantasy art come straight from your imagination, so when drawing your witch or wizard, you can be as creative as you want No one can tell you that your witch is too ugly or that your wizard is too old. Just follow the basic rules of anatomy and perspective and leave the rest to your imagination!

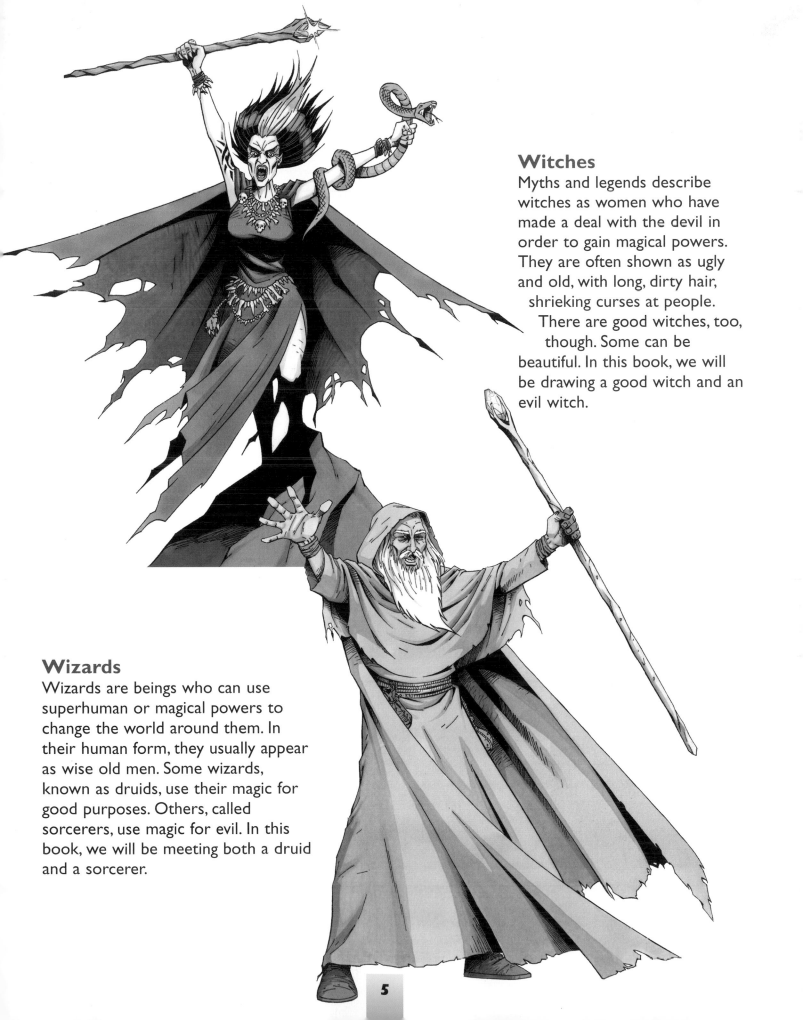

Witches

Myths and legends describe witches as women who have made a deal with the devil in order to gain magical powers. They are often shown as ugly and old, with long, dirty hair, shrieking curses at people.

There are good witches, too, though. Some can be beautiful. In this book, we will be drawing a good witch and an evil witch.

Wizards

Wizards are beings who can use superhuman or magical powers to change the world around them. In their human form, they usually appear as wise old men. Some wizards, known as druids, use their magic for good purposes. Others, called sorcerers, use magic for evil. In this book, we will be meeting both a druid and a sorcerer.

Equipment

In order to create the best possible drawings, you need to start with good materials and equipment.

Paper

For practice sketches, any cheap paper will do. When you move on to ink drawing, however, be sure to use line art paper. You can buy line art paper from an art or craft shop.

You should use watercolor paper for painting with watercolors. There are many weights and sizes of watercolor paper from which to choose.

Pencils

It is important to have a few types of pencils when you begin to draw. Hard-lead pencils last for a long time and will not leave many smudges on your paper. Soft-lead pencils leave darker marks on the paper and they wear down more quickly. Number 4 pencils are the best choice for beginners.

When doing detailed work, be sure to use a mechanical pencil. These are available in a range of lead thicknesses, but 0.5 mm is a good middle range.

Pens

You should use a ballpoint or a simple dip pen and nib for inking. For coloring, you can experiment with the different types of felt-tip pens on the market.

Markers
Markers are really handy pens. Practice using them to get the results you want.

Brushes
You might want to try using a fine brush for inking line work. It is more difficult than using a pen, but many artists prefer it. To get good results, you will need to use high-quality sable brushes.

Watercolors and gouache
You can choose from a range of these products, from student to professional quality.

Inks
Use any good brand.

Eraser
The three types of eraser are rubber, plastic, and putty. Why not give all three kinds a try?

A pencil sharpener may also come in handy!

Faces

As with all character drawing, much of the personality of a witch or wizard is found in the face and especially in the eyes and mouth. It is worth spending a bit of time perfecting your techniques in this important area.

Constructing the face

The human head generally fits into a square. Note that the nose and chin stick out slightly. It may help to divide the square into quarters. The eyes generally sit halfway above the center line, with the nose taking up half the depth of the bottom square. Notice where the ears line up in relation to the eyes and nose. This example is based on a standard-size head. With fantasy drawing, it may be necessary to change this formula!

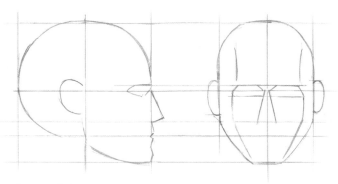

Eyes

These eyes are serious looking but not scary. They might sit well on the face of a druid.

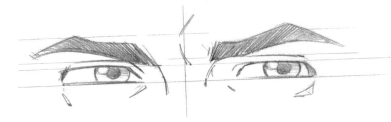

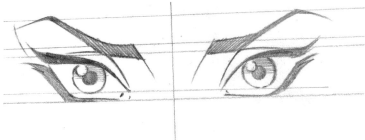

These eyes are clearly feminine, so it is no surprise that they belong to a witch.

Whoa! These eyes are definitely not inviting you over for dinner, unless, of course, you happen to be on the menu! These could be right for a sorcerer.

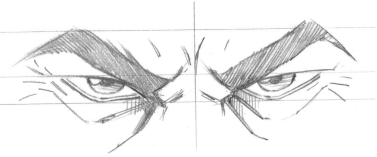

Mouths

Study these simple drawings of mouths. Note how the male and female mouths differ. A simple way of establishing the sex of a character is to keep the mouth of a male simple, without lips, and to draw full lips on a female. It also helps to make male characters' mouths bigger than those of females.

Putting it all together

Now let's try to put together what we have learned and draw a wizard's face. To make it a little trickier, this one is looking down at a three-quarter angle. When drawing wizards' faces, remember they should be old looking as they will have spent a lifetime studying the art of magic. A nice long beard is a good starting point.

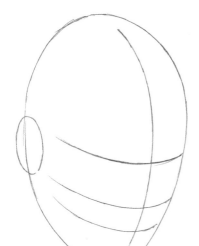

Good Witch

Witches do not have to be ugly. They can use their powers to make themselves appear very attractive, if not beautiful, like this witch.

Stage 1

The pose of this character is unusual because she will be floating and not standing. In fact, she will be appearing from mist. Start with a stick figure to establish her basic shape. Note how the lines come to a point at the bottom just above the crystal ball.

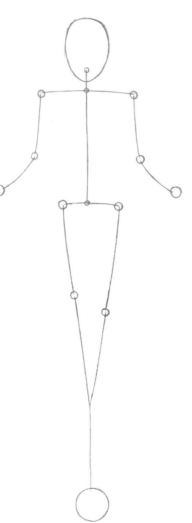

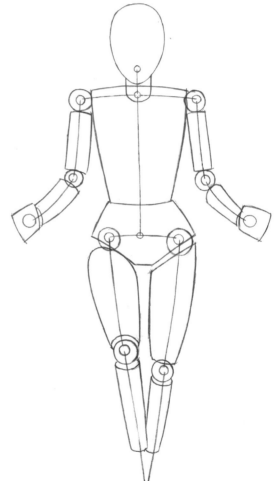

Stage 2

Add body shape to the stick figure. The human form can be constructed from geometric shapes such as cylinders and spheres. Use these to create her head, torso, and limbs. There is no need for feet because she will only appear solid from the knees up.

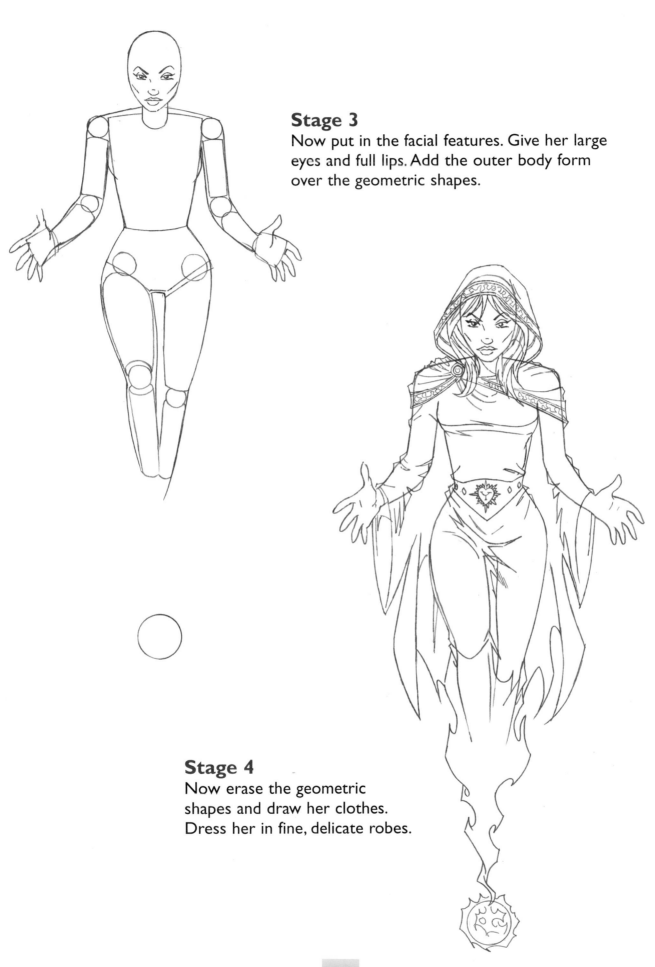

Stage 3
Now put in the facial features. Give her large eyes and full lips. Add the outer body form over the geometric shapes.

Stage 4
Now erase the geometric shapes and draw her clothes. Dress her in fine, delicate robes.

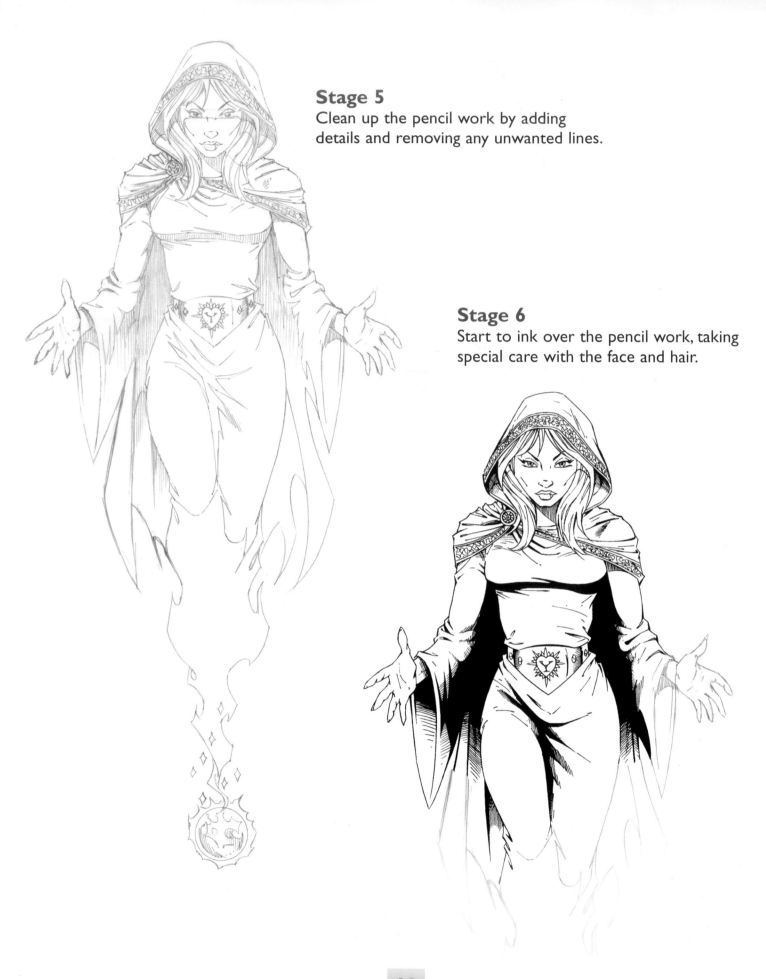

Stage 5

Clean up the pencil work by adding details and removing any unwanted lines.

Stage 6

Start to ink over the pencil work, taking special care with the face and hair.

Stage 7

If you have kept the line work nice and crisp, you should end up with something quite dramatic.

Stage 8

You can color your drawing
using markers, felt-tips, or watercolors.
Lay down each color in one continuous
wash if you can, applying the color as
smoothly as possible. To give depth and
shape to your drawing, apply a second
wash in a darker tone of the same
color range. Make sure the first coat is
completely dry before applying the
second coat.

Evil Witch

Our evil witch should look powerful and scary, with wild hair and outstretched arms, as she summons up the dark forces at her command.

Stage 1

Use the stick figure to create a forceful pose.

Stage 2

Now use the geometric shapes as you did in the previous exercise. Use more slender shapes for a female figure than you would for a male.

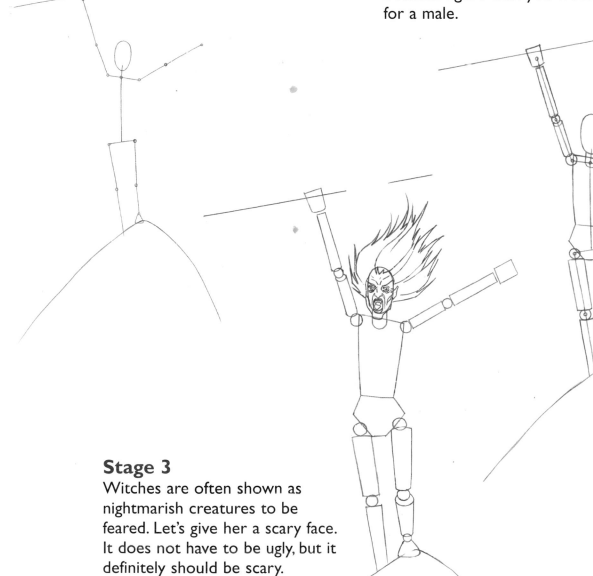

Stage 3

Witches are often shown as nightmarish creatures to be feared. Let's give her a scary face. It does not have to be ugly, but it definitely should be scary.

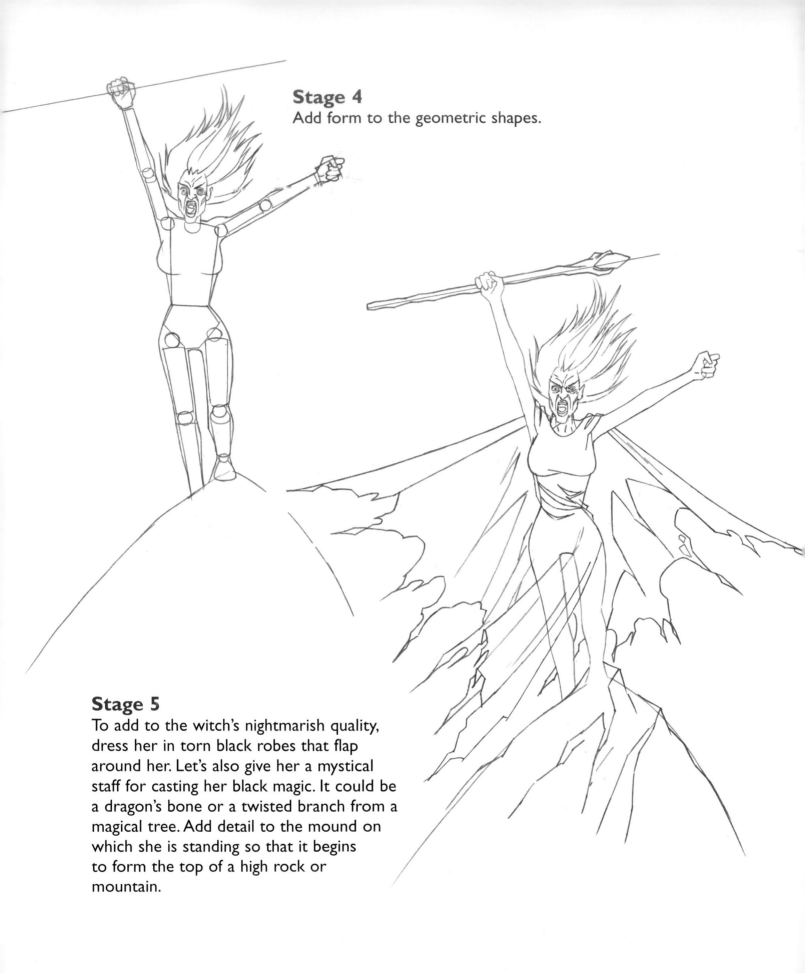

Stage 4
Add form to the geometric shapes.

Stage 5
To add to the witch's nightmarish quality, dress her in torn black robes that flap around her. Let's also give her a mystical staff for casting her black magic. It could be a dragon's bone or a twisted branch from a magical tree. Add detail to the mound on which she is standing so that it begins to form the top of a high rock or mountain.

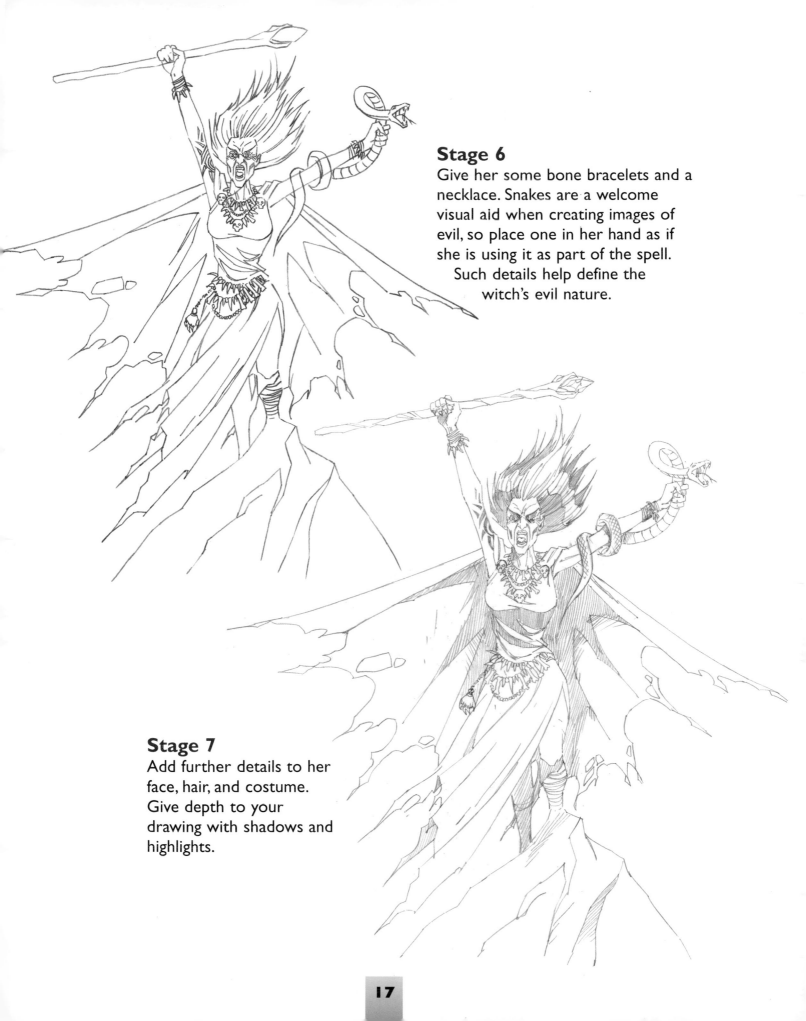

Stage 6

Give her some bone bracelets and a necklace. Snakes are a welcome visual aid when creating images of evil, so place one in her hand as if she is using it as part of the spell. Such details help define the witch's evil nature.

Stage 7

Add further details to her face, hair, and costume. Give depth to your drawing with shadows and highlights.

Stage 8

Once you have cleaned up your pencil
work, start adding black ink. You can use
a brush or pen, whichever you feel more
comfortable using.

Stage 9

If you take enough time
and care over the inking,
you should end up with a
powerful and dramatic
illustration.

Stage 10
Giving the witch pale skin makes the darker areas of the image, such as the eyes and mouth, more intense. You can make the character even more nightmarish by adding a slight green tone to her skin.

Good Wizard

Druids spend their lives working for the greater good. They are devoted to the quest for knowledge, truth, and the harnessing of cosmic energy.

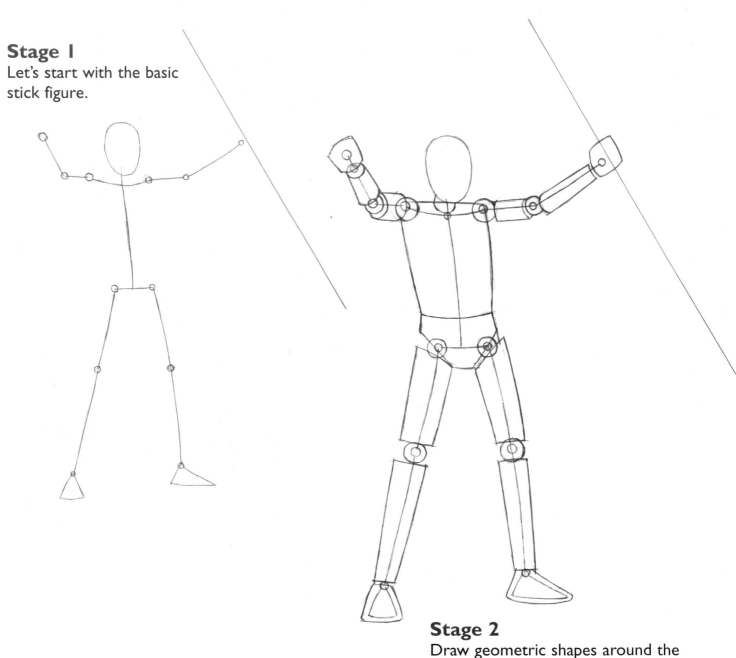

Stage 1
Let's start with the basic stick figure.

Stage 2
Draw geometric shapes around the stick figure.

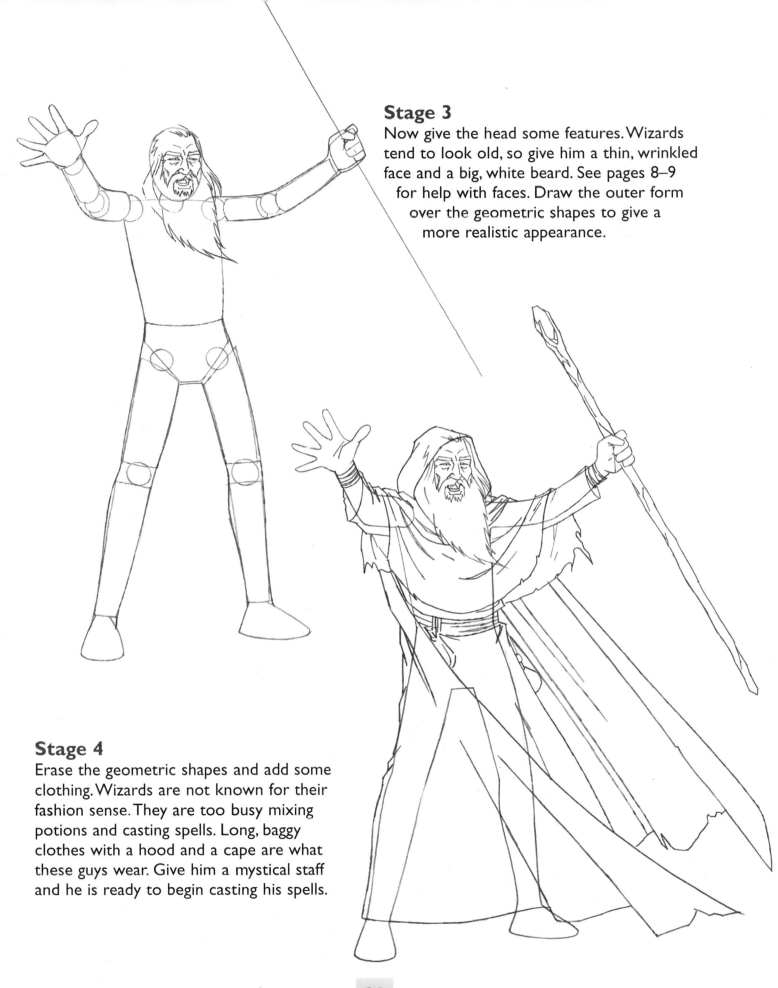

Stage 3

Now give the head some features. Wizards tend to look old, so give him a thin, wrinkled face and a big, white beard. See pages 8–9 for help with faces. Draw the outer form over the geometric shapes to give a more realistic appearance.

Stage 4

Erase the geometric shapes and add some clothing. Wizards are not known for their fashion sense. They are too busy mixing potions and casting spells. Long, baggy clothes with a hood and a cape are what these guys wear. Give him a mystical staff and he is ready to begin casting his spells.

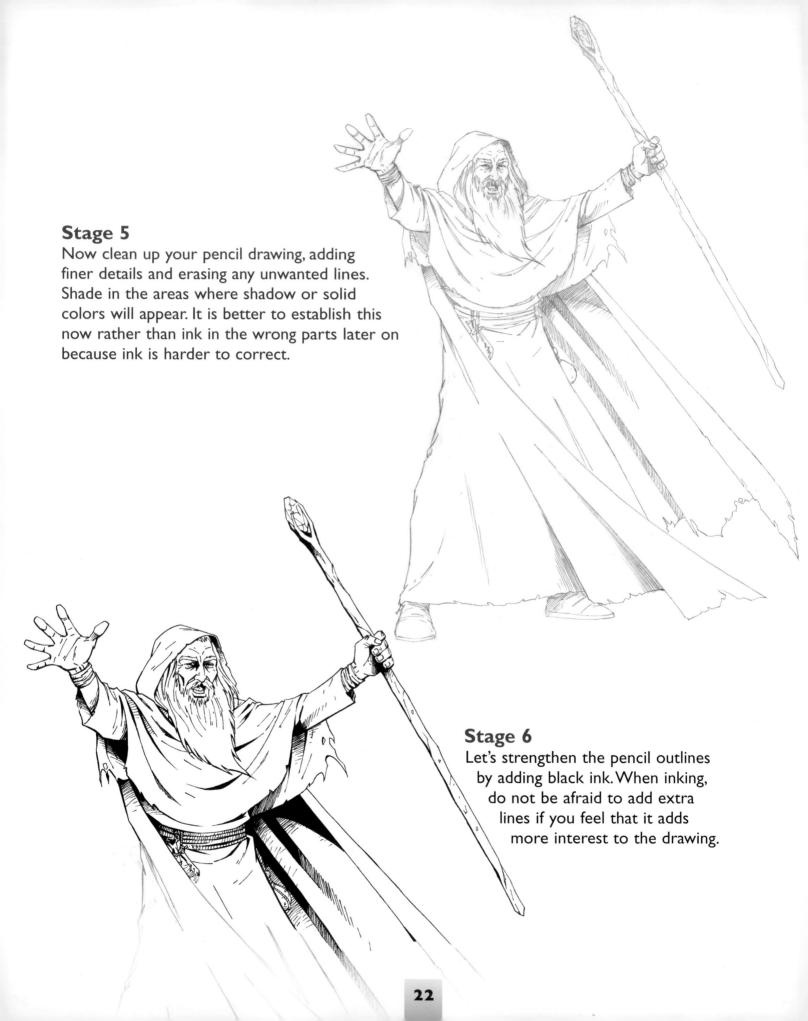

Stage 5

Now clean up your pencil drawing, adding finer details and erasing any unwanted lines. Shade in the areas where shadow or solid colors will appear. It is better to establish this now rather than ink in the wrong parts later on because ink is harder to correct.

Stage 6

Let's strengthen the pencil outlines by adding black ink. When inking, do not be afraid to add extra lines if you feel that it adds more interest to the drawing.

Stage 7
Vary the width of the inked lines to play up the shadows in the wizard's face and the folds in his clothing.

Stage 8

If you want to color your drawing, use a midrange skin tone for the flesh and a light brown for your wizard's clothes.

Evil Wizard

Evil wizards, or sorcerers, use their magic powers to make bad things happen. This particular wizard is definitely not the sort of character you would want to cross.

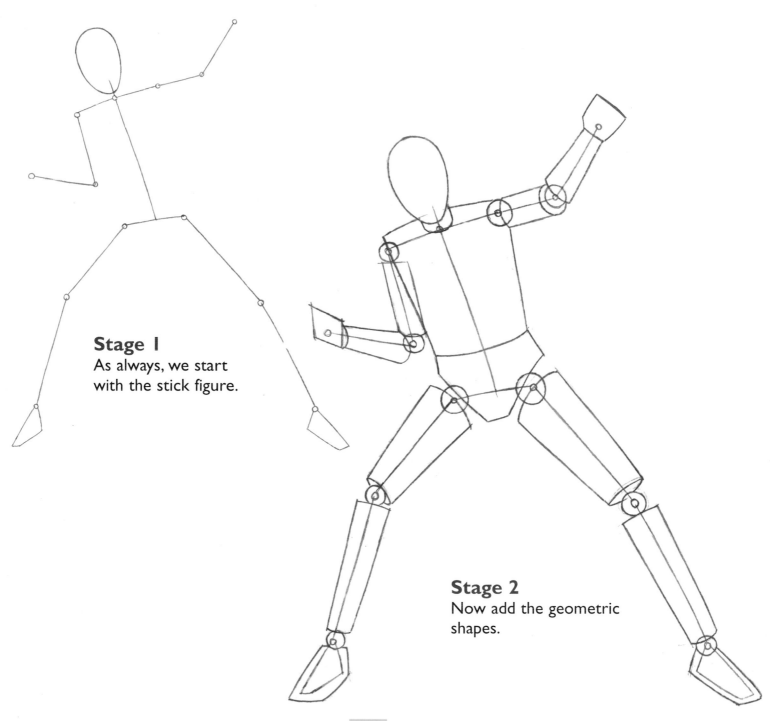

Stage 1
As always, we start with the stick figure.

Stage 2
Now add the geometric shapes.

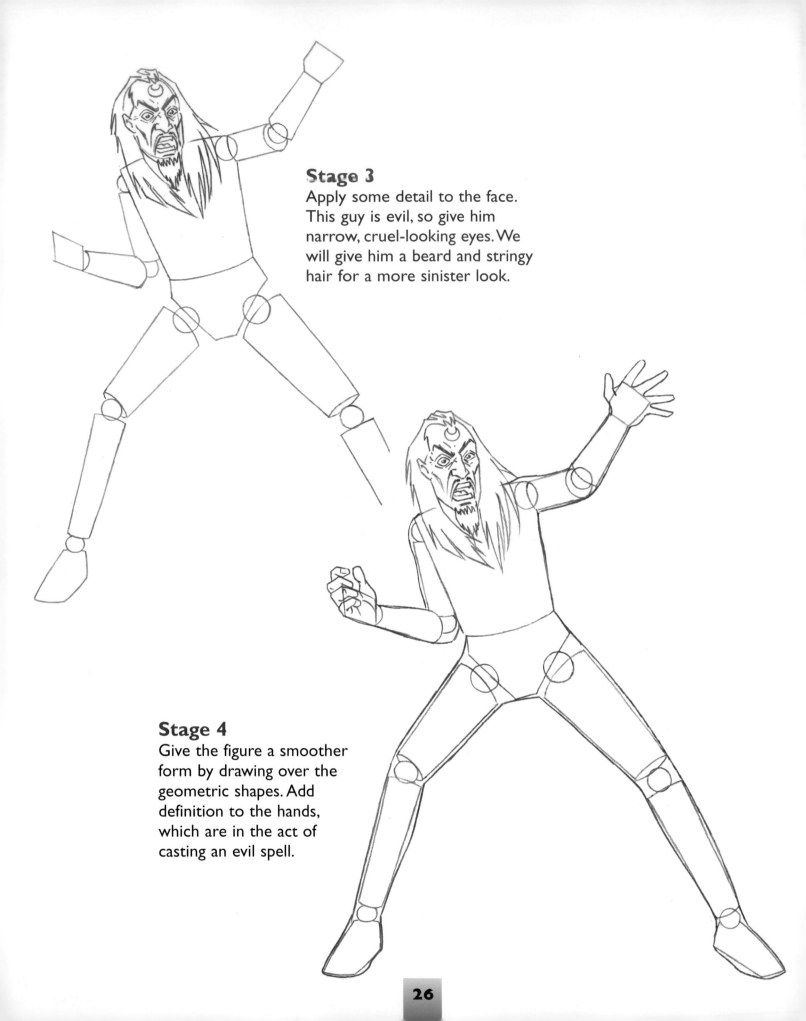

Stage 3

Apply some detail to the face. This guy is evil, so give him narrow, cruel-looking eyes. We will give him a beard and stringy hair for a more sinister look.

Stage 4

Give the figure a smoother form by drawing over the geometric shapes. Add definition to the hands, which are in the act of casting an evil spell.

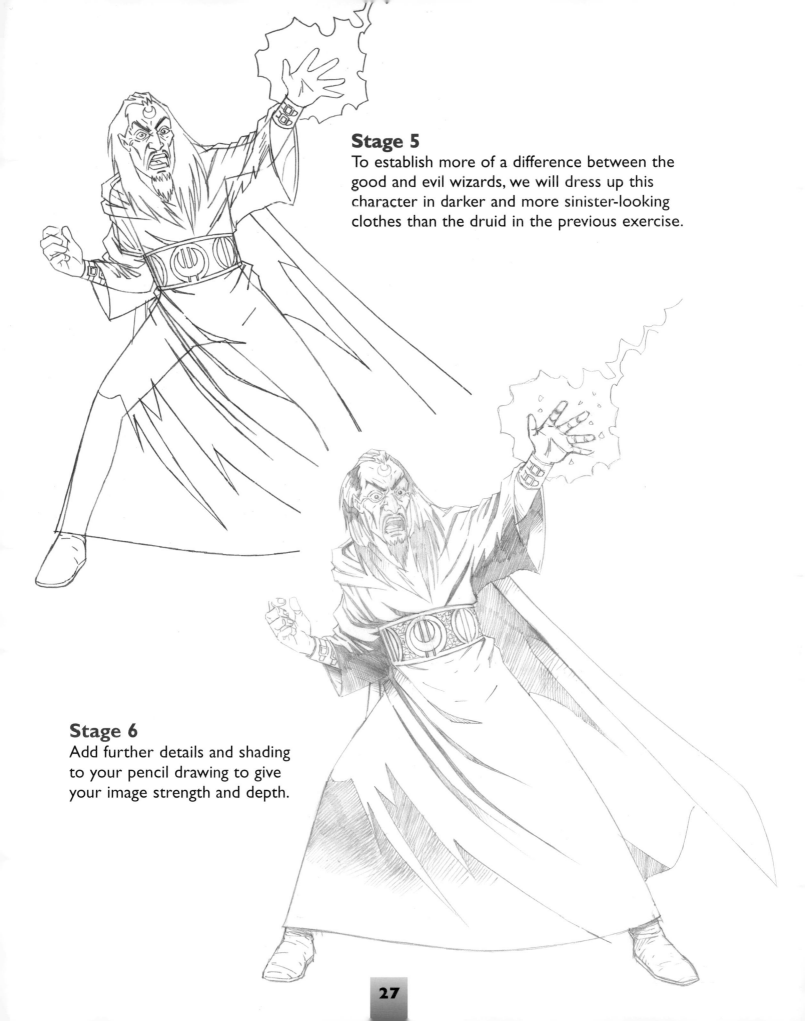

Stage 5
To establish more of a difference between the good and evil wizards, we will dress up this character in darker and more sinister-looking clothes than the druid in the previous exercise.

Stage 6
Add further details and shading to your pencil drawing to give your image strength and depth.

Stage 7
Now start to apply the ink to the line work.

Stage 8
Here we have the finished ink drawing of an evil wizard calling up the powers of darkness.

Stage 9

Color is a useful way of establishing the nature of your character. Dark colors, for example, are commonly used to represent evil in illustrations and movies. In addition to using blacks and grays, you could try adding some dark red and green tones.

Glossary

anatomy (uh-NA-tuh-mee) The physical structure of a human or other organism.

crystal ball (KRIS-tul BOL) A clear solid sphere of glass or rock crystal used to predict the future.

cylinder (SIH-len-der) A shape with straight sides and circular ends of equal size.

druid (DROO-id) A good wizard. Also a priest in an ancient religion who worships the forces of nature.

facial (FAY-shul) Of the face.

geometric shape (jee-uh-MEH-trik SHAYP) A simple shape, such as a cube, a sphere, or a cylinder.

gouache (GWAHSH) A mixture of nontransparent watercolor paint and gum.

highlight (HY-lyt) An area of very light tone in an illustration that provides contrast or the appearance of illumination.

legends (LEH-jendz) Stories passed down through the years, that cannot be proved.

mechanical pencil (mih-KA-nih-kul PENT-sul) A pencil with replaceable lead that may be advanced as needed.

myths (MITHS) Stories that people make up to explain events.

mystical (MIS-tih-kul) Something with supernatural or spiritual significance or power.

personality (per-sun-A-lih-tee) How a person or an animal acts with others.

perspective (per-SPEK-tiv) In drawing, changing the relative size and appearance of objects to allow for the effects of distance.

potion (POH-shun) A drink with magical powers.

sable brush (SAY-bul BRUSH) An artist's brush made with the hairs of a sable, a small mammal from northern Asia.

sinister (SIH-nes-ter) Threatening or menacing.

sorcerer (SOR-suh-rer) A wizard who uses his magic for evil purposes.

sphere (SFEER) An object shaped like a ball.

stick figure (STIK FIH-gyur) A simple drawing of a person with single lines for the torso, arms and legs.

torso (TOR-soh) The upper part of the human body, not including the head and arms.

watercolor (WO-ter-kuh-ler) Paint made by mixing pigments, or the substances that give something its color, with water.

Further Reading

Books

Drawing and Painting Fantasy Figures: From the Imagination to the Page by Finlay Cowan (David and Charles, 2004)

Draw Magical Fantasies: A Step-by-Step Guide by Damon J. Reinagle (Peel Productions, 2002)

How to Draw Fairies and Mermaids by Fiona Watt and Jan McCafferty (illustrator) (Usborne, 2005)

How to Draw Fantasy Characters by Christopher Hart (Watson-Guptill Publications, 1999)

How to Draw Ghosts, Goblins, Witches and other Spooky Characters by Barbara Soloff Levy (Sagebrush, 1999)

How to Draw Wizards, Dragons and other Magical Creatures by Barbara Soloff Levy (Dover Publications, 2004)

Web Sites

Due to the changing nature of Internet links, PowerKids Press has developed an online list of Web sites related to the subject of this book. This site is updated regularly. Please use this link to access the list: www.powerkidslinks.com/dfa/witch/

Index